Contents

Introduction 1

    Digital Age Leadership 1

Overview 3

    ISTE Standards for Students 4

    ISTE Standards for Educators 6

    ISTE Standards for Education Leaders 9

    Themes Across the Standards 14

    Essential Conditions 15

Finding Yourself in the ISTE Standards 16

    Principal/Assistant Principal 16

    Superintendent/Assistant Superintendent 18

    Chief Academic Officers and Chief Innovation Officers 20

    Chief Technology Officer/Chief Information Officer 21

    Higher Education 23

    Professional Learning /Development Staff 24

    Questions for All Leaders 25

Vignettes 27

    Equity and Citizenship Advocate 27

    Visionary Planner 28

    Empowering Leader 29

    Systems Designer 30

    Connected Learner 31

Connecting Leadership Standards 32

    Professional Standards for Educational Leaders (PSEL) 32

    National Educational Leadership Preparation (NELP) 33

    Learning Forward 34

    Future Ready 34

Crosswalk of ISTE Standards for Education Leaders and ISTE's Essential Conditions 36

    Strategic Planning Is Ongoing Work 36

    The Standards and the Essential Conditions 37

Development Team and Credits 39

Introduction

Schools and districts are made up of a diverse and interconnected community of students, educators and other staff. As research develops and new technology tools and resources proliferate, educational leaders are faced with an increasingly complex task as they consider how to provide appropriate, personalized learning for all. Digital technologies are multifaceted tools that educational leaders can leverage to best meet the needs of students. The ISTE Standards for Education Leaders provide a full framework with all the individual components needed for strong, positive systems change for learning with technology in a manageable, easy to follow format.

The standards reflect research-based best practices and developments in education technology and have evolved from the original set released in 2001, the revised 2009 standards and the newest version in 2018. More than 130 people from 50 states and 32 countries were involved in the standards refresh.

The leader standards are not intended to be used alone. Strong leaders also use the ISTE Standards for Educators and the ISTE Standards for Students to bring about holistic change with a shared vision and direction for all. Each set of standards are highly relevant to the educational leader and are collectively used throughout this booklet.

Digital Age Leadership

The digital era demands a need for change in school structure and leadership practices. The traditional model of "school leader as manager" comes from the industrial era and does not have a place in today's schools. Managers of the past developed a controlled environment where students were tethered to their desks and teachers were isolated in their classrooms. Technology has had a disruptive effect on this type of structure as it has opened up the possibility of different types of relationships, interactions and learning (Merchant, 2012).

Schools and districts are historically based on a hierarchical pyramidal structure of power, privilege and access to information. The how, when, where and what should be learned is regulated by national, state and district requirements. However, digital technologies put power in the hands of learners and educators, and great school and district leaders integrate digital technologies to develop a learning landscape that embraces shared leadership, trust and encouragement.

> **Learning is natural, ubiquitous and essential to our humanness.**

The ISTE Standards for Educators provide guidance on how the educator role can shift from one of authority figure to one of facilitator and supporter as educators become learning guides and pedagogical pioneers. The ISTE Standards for Students regard students as reflective, active directors of learning as they become adaptive, creative problem solvers. The ISTE Standards connect with the philosophy that learning is natural, ubiquitous and essential to our humanness (Alexander, Schallert & Reynolds, 2009) and provide a road map for how digital technologies can be effectively integrated into education to empower students, educators and leaders in reaching their learning potential.

The role of the educational leader is paramount in developing a culture of change. It is important that school and district leaders recognize that, rather than managing people through a directed approach, the leader provides the environment, culture and opportunities to nurture and empower educators and students to be self-driven.

From Management to Facilitation

Moving toward student-centric learning is not a new concept. After all, John Dewey promoted the idea in the 19th century. What is new are the many ways digital technologies allow educators to personalize learning. Often change comes from a shift in culture, which is built on the nebulous foundation of traditions, values, beliefs and rituals built up over time. School culture is all encompassing, yet elusive and often difficult to interpret. Nonetheless, the school culture determines the attitudes, beliefs, decisions and actions of educators and students. The ISTE Standards for Education Leaders provide a set of guidelines and examples to enable school and district leaders to move the school toward a positive school culture by promoting equity, change, empowerment, strong systems and connected learning experiences.

It is important to recognize that leadership appears in many forms. District leaders make changes across multiple schools, principals across their schools and teacher leaders within and across grade levels. The top-down model is no longer the only avenue of change. School and district leaders value and encourage expertise and ideas. Great initiatives are now recognized from leadership provided by strong educators with valued experience and knowledge. Change is multidirectional to allow all members of the education community to contribute. Leaders create the culture and conditions for innovation and earn respect by modeling an open policy of leadership.

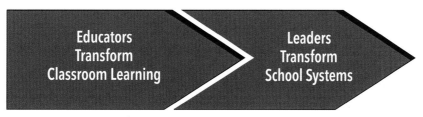

Figure 1. Educators transform learning, leaders transform systems, students reflect those changes with transformative learning.

Alexander, P. A., Schallert, D. L., & Reynolds, R. E. (2009). What is learning anyway? A topographical perspective considered. *Educational Psychologist, 44*(3), 176–192.

Merchant, G. (2012). Mobile practices in everyday life: Popular digital technologies and schooling revisited. *British Journal of Educational Technology, 43*(5), 770-782.

Overview
The ISTE Standards for Education Leaders, Educators and Students and the ISTE Essential Conditions

The ISTE family of standards provides a comprehensive road map to effective technology integration into PK–12 schools. The standards focus on different roles in educational structures that support the individual in best meeting the needs of the learners. Nonetheless, roles do not function independently, and the standards are developed to go hand-in-hand and inform across all roles. For example, the role of leader is not a position only for those at the district or principal level. Teachers take on strong leadership roles, such as grade-level leader and curriculum specialist, and the ISTE Standards for Education Leaders inform all types of educational leaders. Classroom teachers focused on their role as educators will use the ISTE Standards for Educators, but they will also use the ISTE Standards for Students to determine what students should be accomplishing in the classroom with technology.

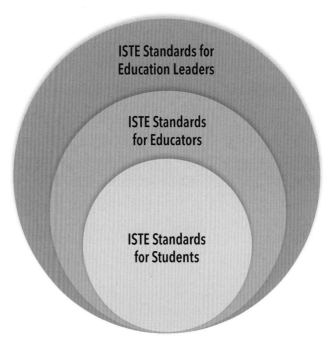

Figure 2. The ISTE Standards for Students are central to the work of educators and educational leaders.

The image in Figure 2 shows the relationship of the ISTE Standards. Students are at the center of this image and the ultimate focus of our educational endeavors. Educators are the second circle and they consider their own standards while also using the ISTE Standards for Students to inform their decisions. The final circle is that of the leader who actively uses all three sets of standards. This leader engenders an educational systemic change from management to facilitation building on strengths and a shared vision with the use of technology.

ISTE Standards for Students

The ISTE Standards for Students (2016) are designed to empower student voice and ensure that learning is a student-driven process. These standards leverage technology to promote the development of student attributes to ensure learning with the goal of cultivating these skills throughout a student's academic career and beyond. There are seven student standards: Empowered Learner, Digital Citizen, Knowledge Constructor, Innovative Designer, Computational Thinker, Creative Communicator and Global Collaborator.

Students are empowered learners who set goals, build networks, troubleshoot and transfer knowledge to new situations. Students are digital citizens who cultivate a positive digital identity modeling positive, safe, legal and ethical online behaviors. Students are knowledge constructors who employ research strategies to find and curate resources and information, evaluate the accuracy, credibility, and relevance of information and build knowledge by exploring real-world issues and problems. Students are innovative designers who use a design process to generate ideas, test theories, create knowledge and innovative artifacts; select and use digital tools to plan and manage design processes; develop, test and refine prototypes and exhibit tolerance for ambiguity and perseverance with open-ended problems.

Students are computational thinkers who collect, select and analyze data and use technology for data analysis, abstract models and algorithmic thinking. Students are creative communicators who choose appropriate platforms and tools for creation or communication; communicate ideas using a variety of digital objects, such as visualizations, models or simulations; and present customized messages and media for various audiences. Finally, students are global collaborators who broaden their perspectives and enrich their learning by collaborating with others and working effectively in teams locally and globally.

1. Empowered Learner

Students leverage technology to take an active role in choosing, achieving and demonstrating competency in their learning goals, informed by the learning sciences. Students:

a. Articulate and set personal learning goals, develop strategies leveraging technology to achieve them and reflect on the learning process itself to improve learning outcomes.

b. Build networks and customize their learning environments in ways that support the learning process.

c. Use technology to seek feedback that informs and improves their practice and to demonstrate their learning in a variety of ways.

d. Understand the fundamental concepts of technology operations, demonstrate the ability to choose, use and troubleshoot current technologies and are able to transfer their knowledge to explore emerging technologies.

2. Digital Citizen

Students recognize the rights, responsibilities and opportunities of living, learning and working in an interconnected digital world, and they act and model in ways that are safe, legal and ethical. Students:

a. Cultivate and manage their digital identity and reputation and are aware of the permanence of their actions in the digital world.

b. Engage in positive, safe, legal and ethical behavior when using technology, including social interactions online or when using networked devices.

c. Demonstrate an understanding of and respect for the rights and obligations of using and sharing intellectual property.

d. Manage their personal data to maintain digital privacy and security and are aware of data-collection technology used to track their navigation online.

3. Knowledge Constructor

Students critically curate a variety of resources using digital tools to construct knowledge, produce creative artifacts and make meaningful learning experiences for themselves and others. Students:

a. Plan and employ effective research strategies to locate information and other resources for their intellectual or creative pursuits.

b. Evaluate the accuracy, perspective, credibility and relevance of information, media, data or other resources.

c. Curate information from digital resources using a variety of tools and methods to create collections of artifacts that demonstrate meaningful connections or conclusions.

d. Build knowledge by actively exploring real-world issues and problems, developing ideas and theories and pursuing answers and solutions.

4. Innovative Designer

Students use a variety of technologies within a design process to identify and solve problems by creating new, useful or imaginative solutions. Students:

a. Know and use a deliberate design process for generating ideas, testing theories, creating innovative artifacts or solving authentic problems.

b. Select and use digital tools to plan and manage a design process that considers design constraints and calculated risks.

c. Develop, test and refine prototypes as part of a cyclical design process.

d. Exhibit a tolerance for ambiguity, perseverance and the capacity to work with open-ended problems.

5. Computational Thinker

Students develop and employ strategies for understanding and solving problems in ways that leverage the power of technological methods to develop and test solutions. Students:

a. Formulate problem definitions suited for technology-assisted methods such as data analysis, abstract models and algorithmic thinking in exploring and finding solutions.

b. Collect data or identify relevant data sets, use digital tools to analyze them, and represent data in various ways to facilitate problem-solving and decision-making.

c. Break problems into component parts, extract key information, and develop descriptive models to understand complex systems or facilitate problem-solving.

d. Understand how automation works and use algorithmic thinking to develop a sequence of steps to create and test automated solutions.

6. Creative Communicator

Students communicate clearly and express themselves creatively for a variety of purposes using the platforms, tools, styles, formats and digital media appropriate to their goals. Students:

a. Choose the appropriate platforms and tools for meeting the desired objectives of their creation or communication.

b. Create original works or responsibly repurpose or remix digital resources into new creations.

c. Communicate complex ideas clearly and effectively by creating or using a variety of digital objects such as visualizations, models or simulations.

d. Publish or present content that customizes the message and medium for their intended audiences.

7. Global Collaborator

Students use digital tools to broaden their perspectives and enrich their learning by collaborating with others and working effectively in teams locally and globally. Students:

a. Use digital tools to connect with learners from a variety of backgrounds and cultures, engaging with them in ways that broaden mutual understanding and learning.

b. Use collaborative technologies to work with others, including peers, experts or community members, to examine issues and problems from multiple viewpoints.

c. Contribute constructively to project teams, assuming various roles and responsibilities to work effectively toward a common goal.

d. Explore local and global issues and use collaborative technologies to work with others to investigate solutions.

ISTE Standards for Educators

The ISTE Standards for Educators (2017) embrace the shift from teacher-driven to student-driven learning. These standards provide pathways for educators to leverage technology to transform teaching and learning. These standards show educators learning alongside their students, and educators leading others locally and globally. There are seven educator standards: Learner, Leader, Citizen, Collaborator, Designer, Facilitator and Analyst.

Educators are learners who set goals, pursue professional interests and stay current with best practices based on research. Educators are leaders who shape, advance and accelerate a shared vision of empowered learning with technology, advocate for equitable access and model good practices for colleagues. Educators are citizens who engage and focus their students in contributing and participating in the digital world by creating experiences, establishing a learning culture, and mentoring students in safe, legal and ethical practices. Educators are collaborators who commit time to working with colleagues and students, demonstrating cultural competency and using digital technology in collaborative efforts.

Educators are designers who use technology to personalize learning experiences, design authentic learning activities and apply instructional design principles. Educators are facilitators whose students reflect the characteristics in the ISTE Standards for Students because they develop a culture of ownership, manage digital learning strategies and model creativity and expression. Educators are analysts who use data to drive instruction with a variety of assessment practices that accommodate for learner needs, provide timely feedback and communicate with all educational stakeholders.

1. Learner

Educators continually improve their practice by learning from and with others and exploring proven and promising practices that leverage technology to improve student learning. Educators:

a. Set professional learning goals to explore and apply pedagogical approaches made possible by technology and reflect on their effectiveness.
b. Pursue professional interests by creating and actively participating in local and global learning networks.
c. Stay current with research that supports improved student learning outcomes, including findings from the learning sciences.

2. Leader

Educators seek out opportunities for leadership to support student empowerment and success, and to improve learning and teaching. Educators:

a. Shape, advance and accelerate a shared vision for empowered learning with technology by engaging with education stakeholders.
b. Advocate for equitable access to educational technology, digital content and learning opportunities to meet the diverse needs of all students.
c. Model for colleagues the identification, experimentation, evaluation, curation and adoption of new digital resources and tools for learning.

3. Citizen

Educators inspire students to positively contribute and responsibly participate in the digital world. Educators:

a. Create experiences for learners to make positive, socially responsible contributions and exhibit empathetic behavior online that build relationships and community.
b. Establish a learning culture that promotes curiosity and critical examination of online resources and fosters digital literacy and media fluency.
c. Mentor students in the safe, ethical and legal practice with digital tools and protection of intellectual rights and property.
d. Model and promote management of personal data and digital identity and protect student data privacy.

4. Collaborator

Educators dedicate time to collaborate with both colleagues and students to improve practice, discover and share resources and ideas, and solve problems. Educators:

a. Dedicate planning time to collaborate with colleagues to create authentic learning experiences that leverage technology.
b. Collaborate and co-learn with students to discover and use new digital resources and diagnose and troubleshoot technology issues.
c. Use collaborative tools to expand students' authentic, real-world learning experiences by engaging virtually with experts, teams and students, locally and globally.
d. Demonstrate cultural competency when communicating with students, parents and colleagues and interact with them as co-collaborators in student learning.

5. Designer

Educators design authentic, learner-driven activities and environments that recognize and accommodate learner variability. Educators:

a. Use technology to create, adapt and personalize learning experiences that foster independent learning and accommodate learner differences and needs.

b. Design authentic learning activities that align with content area standards and use digital tools and resources to maximize active, deep learning.

c. Explore and apply instructional design principles to create innovative digital learning environments that engage and support learning.

6. Facilitator

Educators facilitate learning with technology to support student achievement of the ISTE Standards for Students. Educators:

a. Foster a culture where students take ownership of their learning goals and outcomes in both independent and group settings.

b. Manage the use of technology and student learning strategies in digital platforms, virtual environments, hands-on makerspaces or in the field.

c. Create learning opportunities that challenge students to use a design process and/or computational thinking to innovate and solve problems.

d. Model and nurture creativity and creative expression to communicate ideas, knowledge or connections.

7. Analyst

Educators understand and use data to drive their instruction and support students in achieving their learning goals. Educators:

a. Provide alternative ways for students to demonstrate competency and reflect on their learning using technology.

b. Use technology to design and implement a variety of formative and summative assessments that accommodate learner needs, provide timely feedback to students and inform instruction.

c. Use assessment data to guide progress and communicate with students, parents and education stakeholders to build student self-direction.

ISTE Standards for Education Leaders

The ISTE Standards for Education Leaders reflect the shift from top-down manager to facilitating leader who leverages digital technologies to build a positive learning landscape in their classroom, school, district and beyond. These standards highlight how to develop a system that embraces shared leadership, trust and empowerment.

There are five standards for education leaders: Equity and Citizenship Advocate, Visionary Planner, Empowering Leader, Systems Designer and Connected Learner. These standards describe leaders who increase equity, inclusion and digital citizenship practices through the use of digital tools. They engage others in setting a vision for the institution and a strategic plan while ensuring a cyclical process of evaluation. Leaders foster a culture of empowerment for all as they support innovative thinking. The standards show that leaders work with others to implement, sustain and improve educational systems to support learning with technology. These standards recognize the importance of leaders who seek to continue their own learning in the digital arena.

Standard 1: Equity and Citizenship Advocate

Leaders use technology to increase equity, inclusion and digital citizenship practices. Education leaders:

   a. Ensure all students have skilled teachers who actively use technology to meet student learning needs[1].
   b. Ensure all students have access to the technology[2] and connectivity necessary to participate in authentic and engaging learning opportunities[3].
   c. Model[4] digital citizenship by critically evaluating online resources[5], engaging in civil discourse online and using digital tools to contribute to positive social change[6].
   d. Cultivate[7] responsible online behavior, including the safe[8], ethical[9] and legal use[10] of technology.

---

1 **Ensure all students have skilled teachers.** For example, hiring for or building the quality and skill level of educators to effectively use technology through professional development and support; closing digital usage and access gaps.

2 **Ensure all students have access.** Lead and advocate for equitable and sufficient access; for example, to make devices, bandwidth and online resources available to all students at school, home or public areas through policies, funding, partnerships and collaborations.

3 **Authentic and engaging learning opportunities.** Learning made possible or improved by the use of technology, digital tools and digital resources; for example, by increasing personalization and differentiation, participating in real-time and asynchronous virtual collaboration, and accessing experts and real-world data.

4 **Model.** Intentionally adopt and demonstrate best practices to lead and teach others.

5 **Critically evaluate online resources.** Assess the credibility and usefulness of data, multimedia and other information resources found online for accuracy, authorship, timeliness and bias.

6 **Contribute to positive social change.** For example, use collaborative tools to engage in virtual social action and leverage online strategies, such as crowdsourcing, crowdfunding and social entrepreneurship.

7 **Cultivate.** Model best practices and behaviors; lead, mentor and support others.

8 **Safe use of technology.** Interactions online or with technology that keep you out of harm's way, such as being careful and deliberate about how much and what kind of personal information you release online as well as protecting yourself from scams, phishing schemes, poor purchasing practices and e-commerce theft.

9 **Ethical use.** Interactions online or with technology that align with your ethical code, such as preventing or refraining from engaging in cyberbullying, trolling or scamming.

10 **Legal use.** Interactions online or with technology that are mindful of the law, such as abiding by copyright and fair use laws, respecting network protections by not hacking them and refraining from using another's identity.

Standard 2: Visionary Planner

Leaders engage others in establishing a vision, strategic plan and ongoing evaluation cycle for transforming learning with technology. Education leaders:

a. Engage education stakeholders[1] in developing and adopting a shared vision[2] for using technology to improve student success, informed by the learning sciences[3].

b. Build on the shared vision by collaboratively creating a strategic plan that articulates how technology will be used to enhance learning.

c. Evaluate progress on the strategic plan, make course corrections, measure impact[4] and scale effective approaches[5] for using technology to transform learning.

d. Communicate effectively[6] with stakeholders to gather input on the plan, celebrate successes[7] and engage in a continuous improvement[8] cycle.

e. Share[9] lessons learned, best practices, challenges and the impact[10] of learning with technology with other education leaders who want to learn from this work.

---

1 **Education stakeholders.** Includes a wide range of roles, including educators, staff, parents and students, and also may include community leaders, education experts, business leaders and others whose voices contribute to a successful outcome.

2 **Shared vision.** Work together with common purpose and foresight to visualize the full potential of technology to transform learning and teaching.

3 **Learning sciences.** Interdisciplinary field bringing together research findings from cognitive, social and cultural psychology, neuroscience and learning environments, among others, with the goal of implementing learning innovations and improving instructional practice.

4 **Evaluate progress on strategic plan, make course corrections, measure impact.** For example, build 4. in data collection, benchmarks, metrics and regular reviews to provide evidence that efforts remain aligned with the vision and guide changes in tactics or strategies.

5 **Scale effective approaches.** For example, move successful experiments or instances of innovation from pilot to rollout across a system to accelerate change.

6 **Communicate effectively.** Leverage technology to keep stakeholders informed or to get their feedback; for example, by using online surveys, online communities or collaborative digital work spaces.

7 **Celebrate successes.** Recognize progress made on the implementation of the strategic plan and the impact it is having on student learning.

8 **Continuous improvement.** A process that involves collecting data at regular intervals to inform changes and make strategic plan implementation more efficient or effective.

9 **Share.** Use digital tools and outlets, such as social media, news media, school system websites, digital newsletters or presentations, to communicate with a broader community.

10 **Lessons learned, best practices, challenges and impact.** As the strategic plan gets implemented, reflect on, document and share the status so that others can replicate successes, avoid unintended consequences and inform their own planning.

Standard 3: Empowering Leader

Leaders create a culture where teachers and learners are empowered to use technology in innovative ways to enrich teaching and learning. Education leaders:

a. Empower educators[1] to exercise professional agency[2], build teacher leadership[3] skills and pursue personalized professional learning[4].

b. Build the confidence and competency of educators to put the ISTE Standards for Students and Educators into practice.

c. Inspire a culture of innovation[5] and collaboration that allows the time and space to explore and experiment with digital tools.

d. Support educators in using technology to advance learning that meets the diverse learning, cultural, and social-emotional needs[6] of individual students.

e. Develop learning assessments[7] that provide a personalized, actionable view of student progress[8] in real time.

---

1 **Empower educators.** Create a working environment based on shared learning, teaching goals and distributed leadership that involves transparent decision making, willingness to accept feedback from peers and subordinates, collaboration on establishing policies, and trusting and mobilizing teaching staff to make appropriate decisions.

2 **Exercise professional agency.** Take responsibility for and ownership of goals and learning and work strategies.

3 **Teacher leadership.** Educators who advocate for students, collaborate and share with colleagues, are willing to experiment and take measured risk, and who work with administration to establish strategic directions for the school, especially with regard to curriculum and instruction.

4 **Personalized professional learning.** Opportunities for educators and other staff to identify what and how to learn to meet their professional goals.

5 **Culture of innovation.** Create a work environment that values calculated risk-taking, experimentation and constructive examination of the results.

6 **Meets diverse learning, cultural and social-emotional needs.** For example, provides culturally reflective curriculum, language supports, assistive technologies and personalized learning.

7 **Learning assessments.** Evaluation of student learning that uses technology, including evaluations that reflect student choice and provide evidence of meeting certain competencies, such as e-portfolios or tools and applications that make reflection transparent, allow for peer review, embed questions or surveys and allow for voice or video recording.

8 **Personalized, actionable view of student progress.** For example, tools and applications embedded with real-time learning analytics that provide timely and precise feedback and inform instruction.

Standard 4: Systems Designer

Leaders build teams and systems to implement, sustain and continually improve the use of technology to support learning. Education leaders:

a. Lead teams to collaboratively establish robust infrastructure and systems[1] needed to implement the strategic plan.

b. Ensure that resources[2] for supporting the effective use of technology for learning are sufficient and scalable[3] to meet future demand.

c. Protect privacy and security[4] by ensuring that students and staff observe effective privacy and data management policies[5].

d. Establish partnerships[6] that support the strategic vision, achieve learning priorities and improve operations.

---

1 **Robust infrastructure and systems.** Sufficient bandwidth, network and enterprise software and applications that are able to consistently meet peak usage demands across the organization.

2 **Resources.** Finances, human capital.

3 **Sufficient and scalable.** Able to meet current needs and anticipate and plan for future needs.

4 **Protect privacy and security.** Protect information and data through precautionary planning and actions, such as training to establish and maintain best practices among staff and students, complying with state and federal regulations for protecting student data and privacy, and choosing technology products and vendors that have robust privacy policies and security capabilities.

5 **Data management policies.** A set of data privacy laws and best practices to maintain vigilance in the face of innovations in cybercrime.

6 **Establish partnerships.** Cultivate useful connections with other school systems; local businesses and leaders; political leaders and staff; and/or companies, nonprofits, and other service providers.

Standard 5: Connected Learner

Leaders model and promote continuous professional learning for themselves and others. Education leaders:

a. Set goals to remain current on emerging technologies[1] for learning, innovations in pedagogy[2] and advancements in the learning sciences[3].

b. Participate regularly in online professional learning networks[4] to collaboratively learn with and mentor other professionals.

c. Use technology to regularly engage in reflective practices[5] that support personal and professional growth.

d. Develop the skills needed to lead and navigate change[6], advance systems[7] and promote a mindset of continuous improvement[8] for how technology can improve learning.

---

1 **Emerging technologies.** For example, new software, applications, tools and devices that can be used for educational purposes.

2 **Innovations in pedagogy.** Teaching methods and instruction that are improved by the use of technologies.

3 **Learning sciences.** As research provides new information about how we learn, examine and implement how those findings can be applied with the system's educators and students.

4 **Professional learning networks.** Virtual avenue for connecting with others to improve professional skills.

5 **Reflective practices.** Think about your actions, your motivations and the outcomes, and then plan for future endeavors in an effort to learn and improve.

6 **Skills needed to lead and navigate change.** For example, building buy-in, listening, mentoring, providing opportunities for everyone to contribute, keeping vision and priorities at the forefront of stakeholders' thinking, breaking down silos.

7 **Advance systems.** Decisions about how to prioritize and sequence change based on opportunities and dependencies within the system.

8 **Mindset of continuous improvement.** For example, resilience, persistence, tolerance for uncertainty, willingness to learn, openness to feedback.

Themes Across the Standards

The standards show the characteristics and qualities that a person in each role will demonstrate, such as designer, leader, learner. Each set of ISTE Standards was developed with the goal of effectively incorporating technology into PK–12 schools While each set of standards is different, common themes connect all three sets. Also, there are many interconnected characteristics across the standards that appear slightly different depending on the role but still hold true to the core qualities that each person will emulate. These characteristics include:

Learner	**Creator**
Leader	**Goal-Setter**
Collaborator	**Equitable Agent**
Digital Citizen	**Advocate**
Designer	**Research-Based Practitioner**

Learners. Students are empowered learners who take an active role in choosing, achieving and demonstrating competency. Educators are learners who continue to improve their practice by learning from and with others as they explore new practices to improve student learning. Leaders are connected learners as they model and promote continuous learning for themselves and others. All learners are self-driven **goal-setters**, **creators** of new knowledge and learning artifacts and **designers** of learning experiences.

Leaders. Leadership comes from many people in different roles. Administrators are charged with being empowering leaders. This leader looks for expertise in others to empower that person to lead using their strengths. The educator seeks out opportunities to lead others and support students to be empowered leaders themselves. The Student Standards encourage students to assume various roles as global collaborators and to lead their peers by demonstrating good digital practices. All leaders are **informed by research** to make strong choices.

Collaborators. If we rely only on the knowledge we personally hold, our work is limited. When we collaborate, our knowledge is amplified and learning happens. Collaboration is crucial for all roles. This is highlighted in the names of the standards, such as Global Collaborator in the ISTE Standards for Students and Collaborator in the ISTE Standards for Educators. However, collaboration is woven throughout each standard and set of standards. For example, education leaders cannot effect change without collaboration; educators cannot learn without collaboration and students cannot gain the skills to become creative communicators without collaboration.

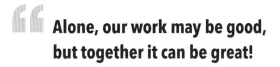

Alone, our work may be good, but together it can be great!

Digital Citizens. In every role, we are all citizens of a digital world. This is a strong thread throughout the standards because we must model and advocate for safe, legal and ethical digital practices. Students of all ages recognize the rights, responsibilities and opportunities of living, learning and working in an interconnected digital world. Educators inspire students to positively contribute to and responsibly participate in the digital world. Leaders model and promote digital citizenship in their schools and districts while embodying the characteristic of equity champion. All digital citizens are **equitable** in their decisions, actions and interactions.

Integration Across the ISTE Standards

Highlighting the interconnections between the ISTE Standards, it is important to note that the Educator and Leader standards specifically make reference to the other standards as they call on a multi-standards approach to effective integration. School and district leaders use the ISTE Standards for Students and the ISTE Standards for Educators as they become empowered leaders, and educators directly connect with the ISTE Standards for Students to become effective facilitators of learning.

Essential Conditions

For effective technology integration, PK–12 schools must conduct a multifaceted approach in considering various elements that collectively will ensure success. For example, a school with access to a wide range of digital equipment might not be successfully implementing that technology if the educators are lacking professional development to use the tools for learning, or if school policies do not align to a digital supported environment.

Determining what critical elements are necessary can be difficult. ISTE has developed the Essential Conditions, a comprehensive framework of 14 robust critical elements that provide education leaders and educators a research-based framework to guide implementation of the ISTE Standards.

The Essential Conditions are reciprocal with the community they serve as:

- Stakeholders are informed by the Essential Conditions.
- Essential Conditions are informed by feedback and findings from the stakeholders.

The 14 Essential Conditions are: shared vision, empowered leaders, implementation planning, consistent and adequate funding, equitable access, skilled personnel, ongoing professional learning, technical support, curriculum framework, student-centered learning, assessment and evaluation, engaged communities, support policies and supportive external context.

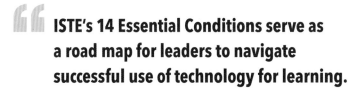

ISTE's 14 Essential Conditions serve as a road map for leaders to navigate successful use of technology for learning.

The Essential Conditions will be mentioned at various places throughout this guide. For a deeper dive, find an overview and crosswalk between the Essential Conditions and other systems frameworks at the end of this book.

Finding Yourself in the ISTE Standards

In this section, you'll find examples of how specific leadership roles use the ISTE Standards in their work. Even though this section is divided by role, exploring all of the content may yield ideas under a different leadership title that works for you. In aligning yourself to the ISTE Standards for Education Leaders, this section will support you in becoming a strong leader who also uses the ISTE Standards for Educators and the ISTE Standards for Students to ensure a holistic transformation of teaching and learning across your school and district.

Reflective questions at the end of this section will guide your thinking about issues you can address in your specific role. These questions draw on the ISTE Standards while also connecting to individual responsibilities related to each job title. Don't try to take on too many questions at once! Rather, reflect and act on these questions one at a time. It is best to do one thing well and build on that achievement.

The ISTE Standards will point you toward successful systems, staff empowerment and capacity building and will help you build confidence in staff and get buy-in for a shared vision.

Principal/Assistant Principal

Principals and assistant principals can use the ISTE Standards in a variety of ways for positive systems change at the building level. This will come from the collective use of the ISTE Standards for Education Leaders, Educators and Students to ensure a sustainable systemic change consistent throughout the school.

The ISTE Standards for Education Leaders provide concrete strategies that building leaders should pursue. Each of the five standards are followed by a list of indicators illustrating specific goals a leader should aspire to. For example, in order for a school to progress, constant change is necessary. While all the Education Leader Standards provide guidance toward positive growth, Indicator 2.a describes the crucial step of developing and implementing a shared vision by engaging stakeholders. The next indicator describes the process for developing a strategic plan from that shared vision. This is followed by evaluating and revising content and practices.

It is all too easy to purchase new technology that seems fun or promising, distribute it to educators and hope that this will bring about positive change. This plan rarely works, however, because technology itself is only a tool. Technology purchases should be based on thoughtful reasoning and involve educators and other stakeholders in the decision-making process. By using the ISTE Standards for Education Leaders, you can avoid such purchasing pitfalls. The ISTE Standards for Educators are another crucial tool for building leaders. These standards outline what teachers can do to bring about positive change in their classrooms. These are not intended to be used to evaluate teachers, but instead provide a set of aspirational goals to set educators in the right direction. Building leaders can adopt these standards to provide guidance to teachers and support them in developing positive digital pedagogy. Technology can be a challenge for some educators and the standards provide guidance and help build their confidence with digital tools.

The ISTE Standards for Students are just as important, and building leaders can use them to understand what meaningful use of technology for learning looks like and to guide and inspire the school's educators.

As a building leader, here are some reflective questions that will help you best use the ISTE Standards at your school.

Principal Reflective Questions

1. Equity and Citizenship Advocate

- How am I ensuring that all students are experiencing equitable, authentic and engaging learning with technology?

- How can I model digital citizenship and the cultivation of responsible online behaviors?

2. Visionary Planner

- How can I contribute to my district/system's development of a visionary plan for technology used for learning?

- How am I deepening the implementation of the shared vision within my school and sharing our successes, innovations and challenges throughout the district and beyond?

3. Empowering Leader

- How do I create leadership roles within my school so that educators can be champions of technology used for learning?

- In what ways am I supporting and empowering educators to meet the diverse needs of all students in the building?

4. Systems Designer

- How am I advocating for educators' and students' technology needs and ensuring that the district is planning for current and future needs?

- What am I doing to ensure that my staff and students follow effective data privacy, management and security requirements?

5. Connected Learner

- How am I allocating resources so staff, including myself, can attend conferences, pursue personalized professional development and learn about the innovative use of technology for learning?

- In what ways am I engaged in learning about new digital tools and pedagogies, including creating time and space to explore and implement new digital tools?

Superintendent/Assistant Superintendent

Superintendents and assistant superintendents can use the ISTE Standards in a variety of ways for positive systems change across the school district. This will come from the collective use of the ISTE Standards for Education Leaders, Educators and Students to ensure sustainable and consistent systemic change.

Mentorship and guidance for leaders comes from many different directions at various levels. That said, guidance for superintendents is not always readily available, and the ISTE Standards for Education Leaders can provide that strong support with concrete examples of strategies. The superintendent is the chief executive officer, who is responsible for a variety of administrative and supervisory responsibilities that vary based on the size of the school district. Regardless of size, there are a number of conditions that superintendents will need to address to be responsive to today's digital society and ensure technology is used to transform teaching and learning across the district. These conditions—known as the ISTE Essential Conditions—are a valuable framework for superintendents to work from. The ISTE Standards for Education Leaders provide more specifics on how to achieve these goals, offering guidance with concrete examples on how to increase equity, inclusion and digital citizenship practices; engage others in establishing a vision, strategic plan and ongoing evaluation cycle for transforming learning with technology; create a culture where teachers and learners are empowered to use technology in innovative ways to enrich teaching and learning; build teams and systems to implement, sustain and continually improve the use of technology to support learning; and model and promote continuous professional learning for themselves and others.

Technology and change can be daunting for many district employees. A lack of knowledge and understanding compounds the stress many educators experience during times of change. Superintendents can avoid creating undo anxiety by adopting the ISTE Standards, which provide goals and strategies for educational leaders, educators and students. Regardless of technological knowledge and abilities, the standards provide a framework for all staff to set goals and work toward successful integration.

As a superintendent/assistant superintendent, here are some reflective questions that will support you in using the ISTE Standards across your district.

Superintendent/Assistant Superintendent Reflective Questions

1. Equity and Citizenship Advocate

- Do my district's policies and procedures speak to equity, and do I provide equitable and culturally relevant resources to all students and educators?

- How am I demonstrating responsible online behavior while also encouraging the use of digital tools for positive social change?

2. Visionary Planner

- What framework am I using to engage stakeholders at all levels in developing, implementing, analyzing and iterating a shared vision for using technology to improve student success?

- How am I showcasing how technology improves student learning, district efficiencies and culture to employees, students, parents and the local and global community?

3. Empowering Leader

- What measures have I taken to foster dispersed leadership, empowering teachers to plan, implement, reflect, fail, celebrate, refine and share their learning with technology experiences?

- In what ways am I creating a culture that includes time and space for exploration and innovation throughout our learning community?

4. Systems Designer

- How do I ensure that a vision and plan for effective use of technology for learning is succeeding throughout the system?

- How am I strategically building partnerships to ensure adequate resources that support the strategic vision, achieve learning priorities and improve operations?

5. Connected Learner

- What online professional learning networks do I participate in to improve my own practice?

- What specific daily actions could I take that would help demonstrate the high expectations of our community's shared vision more effectively?

Chief Academic Officers and Chief Innovation Officers

Chief academic officers and chief innovation officers (CAOs/CInOs) can use the ISTE Standards in a variety of ways for positive pedagogical change across the school and district. This will come from the collective use of the ISTE Standards for Education Leaders, Educators, and Students to ensure consistent, sustainable systemic change.

CAOs/CInOs are responsible for ensuring robust academic systems that support student and educator success. The ISTE Standards for Education Leaders provide the road map needed to meet these targets. For example, Standard 1 can support you in thinking about resources and policies to support equitable, inclusive access as well as to foster positive digital citizenship practices.

Transforming systems with innovative thinking is particularly supported by Standards 2 and 4. Standard 2 emphasizes the necessity of an ongoing cyclical approach to evaluating progress, developing and implementing strategic plans and reflecting and revising those plans. This process is informed by research from the learning sciences to best understand what can be achieved and how. Becoming a Systems Designer (Standard 4) provides direction in how to build teams and systems to drive and sustain innovative transformative change. Standard 5, Connected Leader, will support you in staying informed so you continue learning to use current, relevant information to best effect change in schools.

To understand educator best practices for effectively integrating technology, the CAO/CInO use both the ISTE Standards for Educators and the ISTE Standards for Students. This provides a double-sided perspective as the Educator Standards show the technology goals educators can work toward, and the Student Standards reflect what students will be able to demonstrate when technology is used effectively in the classroom. As part of the systems change, the chief academic officers and chief innovation officers will advocate for the use of the ISTE Standards in schools to provide guidance to school leaders and educators in how they will integrate technology to drive change.

As an academic and curricular leader, here are some reflective questions that will support you in using the ISTE Standards in your school and/or district.

CAO/CInO Reflective Questions

1. Equity and Citizenship Advocate

- How am I demonstrating responsible online behavior and encouraging the development of curriculum and learning opportunities that support positive social change?

- How am I prioritizing and advocating for the closure of equity gaps in my school/district/system?

2. Visionary Planner

- How can I strengthen the connection between curricular and learning initiatives to ensure pedagogical practices are informed by the learning sciences?

- How am I proactively reporting progress toward learning goals and sharing best practices, challenges and lessons learned throughout the larger learning community?

3. Empowering Leader

- How can I improve how the data gathered by my district/system is used to make progress toward learning goals?

- How am I ensuring that the schools in my district are using the tools provided as well as experimenting with new technologies to enhance instruction and empower student learners?

- What have I done to establish a procedure to empowered curriculum teams to evaluate digital content (OER or otherwise) and assess its effectiveness within our curriculum and instruction?

4. Systems Designer

- What processes do I use when implementing new digital resources and curriculum, and do they meet industry best practices?

- How do I evaluate the impact of new technologies on the learning culture and support effective implementation process?

5. Connected Learner

- As a CAO/CInO, in what ways am I both an expert and open to new ideas in technology, digital pedagogy and the learning sciences?

- How do I find and contribute to professional learning communities that will support my own professional goals around technology in education?

Chief Technology Officer/Chief Information Officer

Chief technology officer/chief information officer (CTO/CIO) leaders can use the ISTE Standards in a variety of ways for positive systems change across the school and district. This will come from the collective use of the ISTE Standards for Education Leaders, Educators and Students to ensure consistent, sustainable systemic change.

In your leadership role, decisions are visible to all and change the systems, routines and procedures of those in the education community. Decisions need to be carefully and strategically developed based on research-based best practices and analyzing what is already in place. When implementing digital technology initiatives in school districts, you need to create robust structures and build capacity. CTOs and CIOs must consider equity and inclusion, as well as safe, legal and ethical use of technology. The ISTE Standards for Education Leaders connect all the puzzle pieces together so you can see the whole picture.

ISTE's Standards for Educators and Students are equally important for leaders in this role. Because they focus on teaching and learning transformed by technology, they both guide decisions around what technology to implement and remind leaders that the "why" of education technology is to improve student learning.

As a technology leader, here are some reflective questions that will support you in using the ISTE Standards in your school and/or district.

CTO/CIO Reflective Questions

1. Equity and Citizenship Advocate

- How can I further support district efforts to provide students with connectivity and access to technology tools?

- How do my own practices model responsible online behavior as part of a digital community, including the safe, ethical and legal use of technology?

2. Visionary Planner

- How am I leveraging existing and emerging technologies to support the organization's vision for transforming learning?

- Who are my collaborative partners in analyzing data, providing support and making adjustments to the organization's plan for digital learning, and how am I communicating these efforts out to the broader community?

3. Empowering Leader

- What technologies am I using to model continuous learning, professional agency, innovation and collaboration?

- How are the district/system's technology solutions supporting educators as they meet the diverse learning, cultural and social-emotional needs of their students?

4. Systems Designer

- How am I procuring technology devices and infrastructure for teachers and students to effectively support learning goals and needs?

- How can I continue to improve security and education around data practices for employees and students?

5. Connected Learner

- How do I support professional learning communities (PLCs) to stay current with technology and learning innovations that are coupled with best practices, cautions and lessons learned?

- As a CIO/CTO, in what ways am I both an expert and open to new ideas in technology solutions used in curriculum and learning?

Higher Education

Those in higher education (HE) leader preparation and teacher preparation can use the ISTE Standards in a variety of ways for positive HE systems change. This will come from the collective use of the ISTE Standards for Education Leaders, Educators and Students.

HE faculty can use the ISTE Standards to guide their own work in how they use technology for their teaching and as a framework to align university program organization and content. The standards provide a robust framework to share with HE students who are studying within educational leadership programs and/or teacher preparation programs. The standards offer a concrete set of goals to aspire to and indicators that provide examples of how they can accomplish these goals. These standards are for students studying at the undergraduate, masters and Ph.D./Ed.D. levels.

Effective leader preparation programs will adopt and use all the ISTE Standards, which support sustainable systemic change that cascades down from the ISTE Standards taught at the university, and flows down into districts, schools and to the individual learners. It is important for future leaders and teachers to understand that they can use digital tools effectively to provide transformative learning experiences that prepare students for the digital environments they will face in the future. Leaders use these tools to perform administrative tasks with more reliability, speed and accuracy than without technology, which is crucial for today's school and district leaders. The standards guide leaders through school systems change, equitable access and evaluation. In addition, the standards are organized around characteristics of effective digital leaders.

Effective teacher preparation programs will adopt the ISTE Standards for Educators and ISTE Standards for Students in order to give preservice and practicing teachers a deep understanding of how to effectively integrate technology into the curriculum. This includes specifically addressing key issues, such as being proactive digital citizens to ensure ethical, legal, safe and responsible behavior, how to design and facilitate transformative learning experiences, and how to be an effective collaborator and learner.

HE instructors can use the ISTE Standards for both Education Leaders and Educators to highlight aspirational goals that will lead to thoughtful leadership and lifelong learning. They also underscore the value of keeping up-to-date with research-based best practices to inform their work and demonstrate how fostering a culture of personal agency can engender shared leadership based on empowerment and trust.

In the role of faculty preparing education leaders and/or teachers, here are some reflective questions that will support you in using the ISTE Standards at your university and with your students:

Higher Ed Reflective Questions

1. Equity and Citizenship Advocate

- On my campus, how do I advocate for equitable access to technology for learning and innovative learning practices in all content areas?
- How do I advocate for digital literacy and digital citizenship to be taught across all majors and specializations?

2. Visionary Planner

- How can I support, further or deepen a campuswide vision for technology used for learning?
- What am I doing to promote and adopt the ISTE Standards for Educators as program learning objectives in preservice and in-service teacher education and in educational leadership courses?

3. Empowering Leader

- How can I and my colleagues in higher education better structure courses to allow for personalization, individual professional development and exploration of technology tools relevant to each learner's role or goals?

- How do I empower my colleagues by sharing tips on best practices for blended learning and building teacher presence in online courses?

4. Systems Designer

- How am I having HE education students use the ISTE Standards to help them make systemic choices that are sustainable and informed by research or best practices?

- What are the implications for my students as they become educators or education leaders if they have not been exposed to the effective use of technology for learning in the academic context?

5. Connected Learner

- How do I participate in online networks that share research on innovative learning practices for my own professional learning and share my own research and practices with my colleagues?

- What steps do I take to stay abreast of the latest research in the learning sciences and innovative learning opportunities?

Professional Learning/Development Staff

Professional development leaders are in a unique and potent position to use the ISTE Standards in a variety of ways for positive systems change across schools and districts. This shift will come from the collective use of the ISTE Standards for Education Leaders, Educators, and Students to ensure sustainable, consistent change.

A key aspect of successful professional development is having clear goals that are understood by all participants. The ISTE Standards offer aspirational goals with concrete examples that are organized by educational roles. This avoids the ambiguity that arises when individuals try to parse out their goals from broad overarching statements that represent multiple people in the educational environment. It is important to introduce the ISTE Standards early in professional development to guide teaching and learning with technology.

You can also use the ISTE Standards to conduct a needs analysis to direct the content of face-to-face and/or online learning. Rather than merely teaching educators how to use a particular program or device, you can focus the learning on developing digitally strong characteristics. For example, professional development of the past focused on teachers learning how to use data analysis programs, such as Excel. Today, in addition to learning how to use technology, strong professional development focuses on becoming analysts—that is, knowing how data drives instruction, exploring various assessments and understanding how to use digital tools to assess learning.

Providing robust, relevant professional development can be challenging in this ever-changing digital world. The ISTE Standards for Education Leaders offer a road map to guide quality, research-based learning to all groups these leaders may encounter. Together with the Student and Educator Standards, these standards also provide a framework that PD professionals can use to model and cultivate best practices in teaching and learning.

As a leader in professional development, here are some reflective questions that will support you in using the ISTE Standards in your school and/or district.

1. Equity and Citizenship Advocate

- How am I leveraging the collective perspectives and strengths of educators to promote equity, inclusion and the principles of digital citizenship?

- How can I deepen our approach to professional learning to ensure that all students have access to educators who know how to use technology to transform learning?

2. Visionary Planner

- How am I using my position to advocate for the development of a strategic plan that includes engagement from diverse stakeholders, best practices in technology used for learning and meaningful methods of evaluation?

- How can I lead efforts to prepare my organization to scale best practices in the use of technology to transform learning?

3. Empowering Leader

- What can I do to increase educator empowerment in their work and provide worthy opportunities for personalized professional development?

- How can I ensure the ISTE Standards for Students and for Educators are embedded into our district's professional development plans?

4. Systems Designer

- How can I ensure that the value of professional learning is recognized and included in systemwide planning and implementation?

- What plans and processes can I shape that account for both current and future needs for learning with technology and include support for teachers and students in knowing and observing data security and privacy practices?

5. Connected Learner

- How do I make time for my own professional learning to stay current on new technologies, digital pedagogies and advancements in the learning sciences?

- What can I do to model for educators and colleagues the use of online professional learning communities and digital resources to personalize and sustain professional learning?

Questions for All Leaders

Here are reflective questions for all leadership roles to ensure effective technology integration. Reflect on these questions in addition to those provided above to capture other aspects of your leadership role. Remember to limit the number of questions you focus on to provide adequate time to ensure effective systems change in your educational institution.

Questions for All Leaders

- How can I initiate conversations about digital equity (both in terms of use and access) and cultural relevance to influence professional practice? How might digital tools support these efforts?

- In what ways do I model the rights and responsibilities of citizenship in the digital world including the safe, ethical and legal use of technology?

- How do I use digital tools and networks to contribute to positive social change and to close gaps in technology access and use?

- In what ways do I advocate for access to technology resources and consistent, high-quality learning experiences across classrooms, schools and systems?

- How am I including the voices of all stakeholders in digital-learning visioning?

- Have I developed a vision, including a process for evaluation, where technology is used meaningfully for learning?

- How am I communicating the collaborative vision on our strategic approach with the learning community?

- How am I developing and cultivating teams of learners centered on promoting the use of technology?

- How do I model and develop the delicate balance between safety and agency in digital communities?

- How do our teacher and administrator evaluation platforms help my team think about using technology as a learning catalyst?

- How am I am I engaging parents in their children's learning with a transparent system that is safe and secure?

- How am I supporting effective collaborations among teams in digital environments?

- How am I providing feedback processes, and do they include underserved and underrepresented populations?

- How do I provide opportunities for the learning community to identify effective and innovative pedagogical practices using technology? What can I do to increase collaboration and experimentation among my staff?

- How am I allocating technology resources in a way that supports student achievement and organizational efficiency?

- How do I use technology as a lever to support change in our learning organization? How am I removing the barriers to change?

- How am I partnering with educational institutions and local community businesses to implement educational technology to improve outcomes?

- How do I know what effective technology use looks like and how do I stay up to date?

- How do I ensure that I am regularly reflecting on how my leadership impacts, both within and beyond my network?

- How am I connecting with online professional networks to support my own professional learning? How do I share that with others within my my organization?

Vignettes

This section provides short vignettes to highlight how a variety of leaders in a diverse range of schools have embodied the ISTE Standards for Education Leaders. These vignettes illustrate how you can use the ISTE Standards to be part of a system change in your own school.

Equity and Citizenship Advocate

Vanessa Monterosa is a program and policy development specialist at Los Angeles Unified School District. This is an urban district with strong technology readiness. Monterosa works in the district office and collaborates with other offices to provide a unified digital citizenship message to faculty, students and parents. To transform practices, Monterosa develops digital citizenship strategies that are informed by the ISTE Standards, Common Sense Education resources and research-based best practices.

Monterosa and her office support Digital Citizenship Week in developing and designing an annual celebration at an elementary, middle and high school throughout the district. As part of this event, high school students lead a panel on digital citizenship topics, and elementary school students perform digital citizenship focused vignettes to their peers.

> "We have a team dedicated to digital citizenship because we recognize that it has an incredibly important role in preparing our students to thrive in today's increasingly digital world. We also focus on digital citizenship from a districtwide perspective because we want to shift the narrative around digital citizenship from an extra activity or side task to one that should be integrated across the curriculum because digital citizenship is integral to a student's college and career success as well. We want to support our schools in creating opportunities for students to develop positive, productive digital footprints that will only enable further success for them once they graduate.
>
> —Vanessa Monterosa, program and policy development specialist

Mark Benigni is the superintendent of Meriden Public Schools in Meriden, Connecticut. This district is an urban, technology strong district with eight elementary schools, two middle schools and two high schools. The Meriden Public Schools also include Venture Academy, an alternative education program for high school students and a College and Career Readiness Center. This district serves 8,600 students with 67 percent minority students and 71 percent receiving free and reduced-price lunch. Benigni is breaking down walls of traditional classrooms to create student-centered learning environments to ensure all students have access to the technology and connectivity necessary to participate in authentic and engaging learning opportunities.

As a district committed to student-centered practices, even the youngest students are learning with technology. Benigni prioritized district resources to implement an elementary 1:1 program at an economically challenged public school. He also developed Tech Buddies, a program where older students teach younger students technology skills. The program addresses the challenge of developing young learners' skills and building relationships through engaging activities.

Visionary Planner

Steven Wall is an academic dean at Oak Ridge Military Academy in North Carolina. His is a suburban school serving 65 students who are just getting started using technology for learning. The majority of the academy's students come with some level of academic struggle, but go on to attend four-year schools. About 25 percent of the student body is international, hailing from Angola, Nigeria, Peru and mainland China.

Wall is working with stakeholders to develop a strategic technology plan and goals that will lead to sustainable practices. As part of this plan, Wall is working collaboratively to choose technology to improve learning, based on the learning sciences. He started by focusing on a couple of technologies that could transform learning, and he's working with his team to investigate their uses and practicality both in the classroom and beyond.

> The first stage of our strategic plan is to identify initial tenets and then develop goals that will lead to long-term and sustainable practices.
> —**Steven Wall**, academic dean

Rhonda Schroeder is a principal at Arthur Elementary School in Oklahoma. Her urban school serves 625 students with medium readiness for using technology. Schroeder has worked collaboratively with stakeholders to develop and adopt a shared vision for using technology to improve student success. In 2015, Schroeder started a 1:1 iPad initiative in the low-income, low-performing school, which soon became a model for others in the Oklahoma City Public Schools.

As part of the shared vision, Schroeder developed partnerships and brought stakeholders together to explore choices and collaborate on decision making. The one-size-fits-all ideology is not acceptable in Schroeder's school, and educators work together to determine what fits best for each educatorand their students. Educators use a variety of learning platforms.

> We set out to achieve major milestones in record time. Our implementation included robust and urgent digital infusion with the best digital age practices.
> —**Rhonda Schroeder**, building principal

Empowering Leader

Mark Gerl is an innovation director at Fulton Academy of Science & Technology in Roswell, Georgia. This suburban school serves 550 students with strong technology readiness. Gerl works with educators in his building to foster a climate of innovation and collaboration, based on the ISTE Standards for Students. He helps educators develop project-based learning strategies and learn game-design concepts for lesson design. During his daily "Innovation Hour," Gerl visits classrooms to record moments of discovery and celebration as he supports educators.

> I'm always on the lookout for new ideas that I'll pass along to teachers, then we'll collaborate on how to design the course to engage the students and spark their creativity. We have an extra hour each day called "Innovation Hour" for project-based learning sessions. An example of the projects is "Engineering the Three Little Pigs" where students make houses out of straws, sticks and bricks and then test them against a hair dryer. The technology used is a wide range of low tech straws and tape to Little Bits electronics and 3D modeling software. I've been a substitute for these projects when teachers are out, a sounding board for ideas and a cheerleader for when it goes better than expected.
>
> —**Mark Gerl**, innovation director

Mick Shuran is a middle school principal at West Middle School in Tullahoma, Tennessee. This small rural school system serves 430 students with medium technology readiness. Shuran wanted to change the traditional professional development mold that many schools use. Instead of presenting the same topic and the same activities to everyone, he wanted to develop a system where educators could personalized their PD experience.

So Shuran asked educators what kind of PD they wanted. After gathering that information, he provided personalized PD for the educators in his school.

> What I wanted to do was create a more personalized experience where adult learners can get what they need (not what everyone else needs). Just like what our kids should be getting.
>
> —**Mick Shuran**, middle school principal

Maureen Skelly is a instructional technology specialist at Ancillae-Assumpta Academy in Wyncote, Pennsylvania. This private suburban technology strong school system serves 572 students grades 1–8. Skelly empowers teachers and learners to use technology in innovative ways to enrich teaching and learning. One of the ways she did this was by creating a teacher-led group to explore using augmented reality (AR) and virtual reality (VR) in the classroom. The seven teachers who comprised the group embraced the topic by diving in and learning with students and professionals.

Skelly also empowered students by creating a "STEM Illumination Day" where seventh grade students used Google Street View, Thinglink, Quiver, Google Expeditions, NearPod and Aurasma to teach and share the experience with students in grades 1–4.

> The empowerment of people is the vision of our school and a driving force for my position as instructional technology specialist. I love people. I love learning. I love people learning. Whether it is a student or a teacher, coding or digital storytelling, the privilege of sharing ideas and developing new ways to learn is a thing I will never tire of. I am trying to instill this same joy and passion in every student and every teacher I work with. I strongly believe in creating "sparks" around the school to ignite learning in every nook and cranny.
>
> —**Maureen Skelly**, instructional technology specialist

Systems Designer

Nancy Sweat is the executive director of PK–12 curriculum and instruction and **Chris Jenkins is acting director of technology at Newport News Public Schools in Virginia.** Theirs is a large school district with 37 schools, five early childhood centers and nine program sites at medium-technology readiness. These two leaders wanted to break the typical silo mentality that happens in many districts to foster a partnership mentality.

In the past this school district followed a typical model that worked like this: the curriculum specialists would write a curriculum document for the educators and then the technology specialists worked with the educators to integrate technology. Sweat and Jenkins transformed that model by bringing together the curriculum and technology specialist teams to collaborate on the curriculum document embedding technology from the start. As educators use the curriculum document, they are informed by both the curriculum content and how technology can extend and enhance learning.

> Beyond just the collaboration sessions, one of my goals for the technology department as a whole is get us out of the 'silo' mentality to which my staff have become so accustomed. Partnering with C&D helps us make the most of our technology budget by focusing on resources that more closely align with the division's learning methodologies.
>
> —**Dr. Chris Jenkins**, acting director of technology
>
> ITCs and C&D have always been collaborative, but this year we strove for more formal collaborative learning with structured curriculum development. We also have leadership changes that encourage and value more collaboration and partnerships. ITCs bring the technology expertise, C&D bring the expertise of the standards, but both groups share an expertise of our classrooms and schools. Together the teams naturally (and professionally) make great things happen.
>
> —**Dr. Nancye Sweat**, executive director of PK–12 curriculum and instruction

Paula Dillon is an assistant superintendent at Barrington Public Schools in Rhode Island. Hers is a technology strong suburban district with six schools serving approximately 3,400 students. Dillon and her team are revising the district technology plan using the ISTE Standards. A task force was developed consisting of representatives from all stakeholder groups including educators, administrators, parents, community members and students. Subgroups were developed based on the following categories: teaching and learning, professional learning, data and privacy, community and infrastructure. The subgroups were charged with conducting a baseline assessment and developing goals aligned to the ISTE Standards for the next five years with supports, resources and actions needed to reach those goals. In conducting the baseline assessment and in developing the goals, the teams determined where the district fell in reaching the indicators outlined in the standards. From this process, the district is developing strategic technology goals that include the language of the standards as measurable objectives.

> Our overarching goal is to purposefully connect the strategies and goals of our district strategic plan with our district technology plan to achieve instructional excellence and deeper learning empowered by technology.
>
> —**Paula Dillon**, assistant superintendent

Connected Learner

Dan Lawson is the superintendent of Tullahoma City Public Schools in Tennessee. This urban school district consists of seven schools and 3,500 students. **Julie Daniel-Davis is the director of instructional technology and innovation at Chattanooga Christian School in Tennessee.** These leaders from separate school districts became connected with each other and with other leaders on social networks. Lawson and Daniel-Davis both use these networks to stay connected and learn from the wider community. These online communities of practice provide a place where both leaders can ask questions, comment and hear the thoughts of other leaders and educators in an environment of learning. They enjoy learning from other leaders who model good practices and keep them up to date on best practices.

> I have found participation in online professional learning networks invaluable in my work as a school superintendent. Early in my career as a school leader, I was limited to access to a small group of fellow leaders in close proximity to my work assignment. My ability to expand access to other resources or ideas was often limited to the published literature or people who met at conferences or seminars. In my work today, I can access immediately the best and the brightest in my professional work and readily expect almost immediate feedback and assistance.
>
> —**Dan Lawson**, superintendent

> It also has become a place to share our successes, edtech finds and to feel a sense of belonging. We find getting out of our own district silos helps each of us in persevering and making the best decisions when hearing how other people/districts are dealing with the same issues. … I take my digital presence seriously as a leader and feel it allows me to work beyond the lives of the teachers and students in my school district by also allowing me to invest in a greater educational good in the world at large.
>
> —**Julie Daniel Davis**, director of instructional technology and innovation

Lisa Davis is a middle school coordinator and teacher at Holy Nativity Episcopal School in Panama City, Florida. This suburban, technology-ready school serves 285 students in grades K–8. Davis is also studying for a master's degree in STEM leadership. Davis uses the ISTE Standards in her leadership role at the school, and the ISTE Standards for Education Leaders are particularly useful for her leadership studies. Connecting to Standard 5, Davis set a goal to remain current on emerging technologies for learning, innovations in pedagogy and advancements in the learning sciences. As middle school coordinator and teacher, Davis is often looking for ways to be a connected learner. To do this she participates in webinars, follows edtech Twitter feeds and reads education blogs. Davis also keeps up-to-date by attending the ISTE conference, where she is able to gather information and resources that she shares with others.

> I have gained so many ideas by attending the ISTE conferences. When our tech team returns from ISTE, we share what we have learned with our fellow teachers through in-service meetings and hands-on tech playgrounds (Osmo, Tiggly, Breakout). The ISTE Standards for Education Leaders promote supporting other teachers in the use of technology, participating in professional development and engaging learners through the use of digital resources.
>
> —**Lisa Davis**, middle school coordinator and STEM leadership master's student

Connecting Leadership Standards

The ISTE Standards for Education Leaders provide a strong framework for leaders to use to digitally transform school systems. These standards can work in tandem with other educational leadership frameworks and standards. This section explains how these other standards connect with and complement the ISTE Standards for Education Leaders.

Professional Standards for Educational Leaders (PSEL)

The National Policy Board for Educational Administration developed the Professional Standards for Educational Leaders (PSEL) in 2015. The PSEL standards provide an overarching framework for education leaders, rather than the digital focus of the ISTE Standards. These are the 10 PSEL standards:

1. Mission, Vision, and Core Values
2. Ethics and Professional Norms
3. Equity and Cultural Responsiveness
4. Curriculum, Instruction and Assessment
5. Community of Care and Support for Students
6. Professional Capacity of School Personnel
7. Professional Community for Teachers and Staff
8. Meaningful Engagement of Families and Community
9. Operations and Management
10. School Improvement

There are similarities to the two sets of standards. Equity is called out in both sets of standards, describing equal access to educational opportunities and the necessity of achieving equity in the digital realm. Other shared values between the standards include giving all stakeholders a voice and an emphasis on ethical practices. PSEL Standard 1 focuses on school vision whereas ISTE Standard 2 asks leaders to engage stakeholders in developing and adopting a shared vision for using technology to improve student success.

Ethical practices are described in both sets of standards. PSEL is geared toward local school-level interactions while ISTE's focus is on the larger digital world. School and district leaders should consider both sets of standards when thinking about the local and the global ethical implications.

One way these two set of standards differ is in how they are used. The PSEL can be used for evaluating leaders; the ISTE Standards are developed as personal aspirational goals for education leaders to work toward and are not meant to be used as an external evaluation tool.

National Educational Leadership Preparation (NELP)

In 2018, the National Policy Board for Educational Administration also developed the National Educational Leadership Preparation (NELP) Standards. The NELP Standards are aligned to the Professional Standards for Educational Leadership (PSEL) but are targeted at levels of leadership and the PSEL are more broadly focused on educational leadership.

The NELP standards were developed for institutions undergoing CAEP accreditation and NELP program review. These standards are designed for use in advanced programs at the master, specialist or doctoral levels. There are two sets of NELP standards: building standards and district standards. Building-level standards are meant for assistant principals, principals, curriculum directors, supervisors and other education leaders in a school-building environment. District-level standards were designed for program directors, supervisors, assistant superintendents, superintendents and other district-level education leaders in a school-district environment.

The two NELP standards are similar, with the major difference appearing in Standard 7 as building-level leaders focus on professional capacity, and district leaders work on policy, governance and advocacy.

Building Standards	District Standards
1. Mission, Vision and Improvement	1. Mission, Vision and Improvement
2. Ethics and Professional Norms	2. Ethics and Professional Norms
3. Equity, Inclusiveness and Cultural Responsiveness	3. Equity, Inclusiveness and Cultural Responsiveness
4. Learning and Instruction	4. Learning and Instruction
5. Community and External Leadership	5. Community and External Leadership
6. Operations and Management	6. Operations and Management
7. Building Professional Capacity	7. Policy, Governance and Advocacy
8. Internship	8. Internship

The NELP and the ISTE Standards are alike in many ways. They both focus on meeting the needs of all learners with a focus on equity, inclusiveness and cultural responsiveness. However, the NELP standards provide a broad overview of educational leadership and do not provide specific guidance on technology integration. The ISTE Standards can be used alongside the NELP standards to provide detailed advice in this area. It is important to note that the NELP standards are designed to be used as performance indicators to evaluate leaders. The ISTE Standards are not an evaluation tool but framework to guide leaders in goal-setting.

Learning Forward

The Learning Forward standards are similar to the PSEL in that they both focus broadly on educational leadership and do not specifically address the use of digital tools to promote learning. However, the Learning Forward standards complement the ISTE Standards in enabling leaders to think about their roles from the larger leadership perspective as well as the digital aspect. There are seven Learning Forward standards:

1. Learning Communities
2. Leadership
3. Resources
4. Data
5. Learning Design
6. Implementation
7. Outcomes

The Learning Forward standards aim to develop capacity for learning and leading and are congruent with the ISTE Standards in that they encourage leadership at all levels to develop a shared vision. Similarities can be found between the two standards.

The Learning Forward Standards are organized around various aspects of educational environments, culture, practices and resources. For example, the Learning Forward Data standard is about student, educator, and systems data collection; analysis; and goal-setting. ISTE's Systems Thinker standard focuses on holistic systems change involving data, resources and leadership. Both standards promote cultivating a culture of shared responsibility, mutual respect and relational trust. The two sets of standards are complementary. The Learning Forward standards focus broadly on leadership and the ISTE Standards focus on the use of digital technologies to develop strong school and district learning systems.

Future Ready

The Future Ready Framework is developed by the Future Ready Institute in partnership with the Friday Institute and Common Sense Media as a structure for digital learning, visioning, planning and implementation to personalize student learning. The Future Ready Framework emphasizes the use of digital strategies to maximize learning opportunities and help schools prepare students for success in college and future careers. The Future Ready Initiative was launched in November 2014 at the White House ConnectED to the Future Convening.

Philosophically similar to the ISTE Standards, the Future Ready Framework focuses on using digital strategies to improve learning. The framework can be used with the ISTE Standards for education leaders to provide a more detailed approach to the role of leaders in this process of change.

The Seven Gears of the Future Ready Framework

The Future Ready Framework (Figure 3) places personalized student learning in the center and is surrounded by seven gears, representing focused topics. The outer edge of the figure illustrates a cyclical process of assessment, refining, vision, planning and implementation. Similar to the ISTE Standards, the Future Ready Framework supports collaborative leadership.

The Future Ready Framework provides an overarching focus on using digital strategies to promote learning. This framework does not provide specific focus for roles within education. The ISTE Standards can be used in conjunction with the Future Ready Framework to provide deeper ideas on the role of the leader, educator and student in that process of change.

The Future Ready Framework 7 Gears

- Curriculum, Instruction and Assessment
- Use of Space and Time
- Robust Infrastructure
- Data and Privacy
- Community Partnerships
- Personalized Professional Learning
- Budget and Resources

Figure 3. Future Ready Framework: https://dashboard.futurereadyschools.org/framework

Crosswalk of ISTE Standards for Education Leaders and ISTE's Essential Conditions

The goal of the ISTE Standards is to drive transformation in teaching and learning—transformation that disrupts traditional models of educational role and practice in favor of models that better fit the needs of students, educators, school leaders and other stakeholders, including parents and workforce leaders. A district's strategic plan serves as the foundation for systematic transformation. Without a shared plan in place, it is unreasonable to expect changes to be systemwide.

Strategic Planning Is Ongoing Work

The Essential Conditions are intended to serve as a framework for guiding discussion around strategic planning for schools and districts. Reflecting on the 14 Essential Conditions and how they relate to your school or district's situation can lead to questions such as:

- Is the vision you have for teaching and learning truly shared across stakeholders?

- Do educators enjoy a professional development program that is ongoing, including regular opportunities to discuss, experiment and learn with peers?

- How do policies remain current with the evolving power of collaborative technologies, such as social media?

The 14 Essential Conditions are grouped into three focus areas: people, policies and resources (Figure 4).

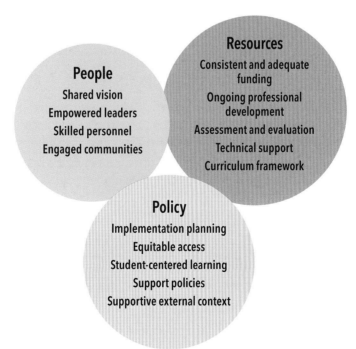

Figure 4. The ISTE Essential Conditions grouped into three focus areas.

The Essential Conditions and the ISTE Standards for Education Leaders complement each other, especially in the area of strategic planning. But while the Essential Conditions offer a framework for exploring these questions, they do not inherently provide educators and leaders a road map or blueprint for how to approach the ongoing work of strategic planning, including implementation, evaluation and revision. One method for approaching this work is through the lens of the ISTE Standards for Education Leaders.

The Standards and the Essential Conditions

There is a relationship between the ISTE Standards for Education Leaders and the ISTE Essential Conditions. For each indicator, there are related Essential Conditions. For example, exploring Equity and Citizenship Advocate, education leaders can articulate connections as follows:

Standard 1: Equity and Citizenship Advocate	
Leaders use technology to increase equity, inclusion, and digital citizenship practices.	
Indicator	**Related Essential Conditions**
Ensure all students have skilled teachers who actively use technology to meet student learning needs.	• Skilled Personnel • Student-Centered Learning
Ensure all students have access to the technology and connectivity necessary to participate in authentic and engaging learning opportunities.	• Equitable Access • Consistent and Adequate Funding • Technical Support • Student-Centered Learning
Model digital citizenship by critically evaluating online resources, engaging in civil discourse online and using digital tools to contribute to positive social change.	• Shared Vision • Engaged Communities • Support Policies
Cultivate responsible online behavior, including the safe, ethical and legal use of technology.	• Shared Vision • Support Policies

Many educators use essential questions to guide inquiry with their students. This helps maintain topical focus and can promote deeper inquiry. In this same spirit, education leaders may ask a set of essential questions that align with each Essential Condition along each standard's indicator. For example, Equitable Access is a pillar of being an effective advocate for equity, especially regarding digital resources, such as hardware and educational applications. This condition encourages stakeholders to examine the following questions:

- Do our schools enjoy 1:1 access? If not, how can we ensure on-demand access to technology for students? Are our teachers using technology to help deliver a consistent learning experience across classrooms?

- How do we ensure that students have adequate connectivity to complete their school work? To what degree are we accounting for inequity in home access?

- Does the technology we've purchased adequately support learners with special needs, including English language learners and students in special education classes?

In a different way, **Student-Centered Learning** is also critical for education leaders to embrace, in order to ensure they hire qualified educators who enthusiastically provide engaging learning experiences for students. This condition encourages its own set of questions:

- How do we use digital age learning standards to define goals for the student learning experience?

- How do teachers use technology to enhance teaching and learning, providing students the opportunities to master academic content and build digital age skills?

- Are our curriculum and pedagogical practices aligned with the learning sciences?

- Do teachers empower their students to develop choose, achieve and demonstrate competency in their learning goals? Do we as leaders support teachers in this effort?

- How do teachers use assessments to describe student mastery in different ways? Do we as leaders support experimental use of new assessments?

- How do we support educators in developing a program for differentiated and personalized instruction that puts student interests at the heart of learning?

These essential questions help guide ongoing discussion and action plans that support each Essential Condition for schools and school systems. Due to the static nature of traditional technology plans, school education leaders should consider adopting a more agile project management strategy for such work. Suggestions for such a strategy include:

1. Keep the strategic plan editable, relatively short and easily accessible to the public.

2. Delegate management of details (such as infrastructure planning, budget management) to respective departments rather than rolling these details up in one document.

3. Maintain a regular evaluation and review process to make sure that the plan adequately captures the organization's position on how technology should be used to redefine learning in the digital age.

Connecting strategic planning with the Essential Conditions and the ISTE Standards helps ensure that education leaders ground the work of leadership in a vision that aspirationally supports the promise of digital age education.

Development Team and Credits

Booklet Author

Helen Crompton, Old Dominion University

Standards Development Team

Richard Culatta, ISTE
Joseph South, ISTE
Carolyn Sykora, ISTE
Sarah Stoeckl, ISTE
Wendy Drexler, Johns Hopkins University
Kara Gann, Smith and Gann Consulting
Annette Smith, Smith and Gann Consulting
David Barr, independent consultant

Technical Working Group

Annette Anderson, Johns Hopkins University School of Education
Gary Brantley, DeKalb County Schools
Doug Casey, Connecticut Commission for Education Technology
Paula Cordoba, San Pascual STEAM Magnet – LAUSD
Theresa Cullen, University of Oklahoma
Christina Garcia, Atwater Elementary SD
Jennifer LaMaster, Brebeuf Jesuit Preparatory School
Dan Lawson, Tullahoma City Schools
Curt Mould, Sun Prairie SD
Julianne Ross-Kleinmann, Dutchess BOCES
Shannon Terry, Arlington Independent Schools

Stakeholder Advisory Council

Bill Bass, Parkway School District
Donelle Blubaugh, SIIA
Julie Evans, Project Tomorrow
Carolyn Gonzalez, Ector County ISD
Violet Hoyle, Virginia Beach School District
Keith Krueger, COSN
Chris Lehmann, Science Leadership Academy
Nancy Lewin. Association of Latino Superintendents and Administrators (ALAS)
Tom Manning Learning Forward
David Ross, P21
Brenda Sherry, Upper Grand District School Board
Cheryl Williams, Former ISTE interim CEO